CHINESE ZODIAC BOOK

CHINESE ZODIAC BOOK THE SECRET ASTROLOGY OF THE ORIENT

By
KIM HAI SONG

 BIPLANE PRODUCTIONS
SIMON AND SCHUSTER

Published by Biplane Productions
8721 Sunset Blvd., Suite C
Hollywood, California 90069
and by Simon and Schuster
Rockefeller Center, 630 Fifth Avenue
New York, New York 10020

First printing

SBN 671-21501-9

Library of Congress Catalog Card Number: 72-93014

Manufactured in the United States of America

Designed by Hy Fujita

CONTENTS

Introduction 11

Chart of the Years 12

Year of the Rat 15

Year of the Ox 19

Year of the Tiger 23

Year of the Rabbit 27

Year of the Dragon 31

Year of the Snake 35

Year of the Horse 39

Year of the Sheep 43

Year of the Monkey 47

Year of the Cock 51

Year of the Dog 55

Year of the Boar 59

INTRODUCTION

All of us at some time have been aware that Orientals were celebrating their New Year—which is a different date than that used by Occidentals. More interesting is the fact that each year is referred to as an animal, rather than a number. 1972, for example, is the Year of the Rat, 1973 the Year of the Ox.

There is a great deal more to this system than the name of the year; for centuries, Orientals have believed that the year in which a person is born has direct affect on his personality.

The Chinese zodiac is divided into 12 years rather than months, the cycle repeating itself every dozen years. It is comprised of the Rat, Ox, Tiger, Rabbit, Dragon, Snake, Horse, Sheep, Monkey, Cock, Dog and Boar.

To learn your Animal Year, consult the chart on pages 12 and 13.

(If born before 1900, simply count in reverse.)

RAT

1900
1912
1924
1936
1948
1960
1972

RABBIT

1903
1915
1927
1939
1951
1963
1975

OX

1901
1913
1925
1937
1949
1961
1973

DRAGON

1904
1916
1928
1940
1952
1964
1976

TIGER

1902
1914
1926
1938
1950
1962
1974

SNAKE

1905
1917
1929
1941
1953
1965
1977

HORSE

1906
1918
1930
1942
1954
1966
1978

COCK

1909
1921
1933
1945
1957
1969
1981

SHEEP

1907
1919
1931
1943
1955
1967
1979

DOG

1910
1922
1934
1946
1958
1970
1982

MONKEY

1908
1920
1932
1944
1956
1968
1980

BOAR

1911
1923
1935
1947
1959
1971
1983

YEAR OF THE RAT

**1900, 1912, 1924, 1936,
1948, 1960, 1972**

You're a go-getter, filled with energy and ambition, and blessed with an imaginative flair. Rat people are that rare combination of ambition and honesty; others instinctively feel they can trust you.

Because you are a perfectionist you are fussy about details; when you finish a job it is invariably well done — the only kind of accomplishment that gives you satisfaction.

Although a hard worker, you are prone to spend too much money on loved ones. In fact, this is the *only* way you spend freely; otherwise you tend to excessive thrift. The majority of Rat people have a fat savings account.

In your striving for the top you are innately careful not to hurt others. This, combined with sound judgment and the luck of a charmed life, enables you to work well with people. You should therefore follow a career involving contact with others.

You are sometimes small-minded and easily angered, and therefore seldom have lasting friendships.

The first part of your life is filled with good fortune. There are hardships in middle age, but in your latter years you will live well—possibly off the fat of that savings account.

You are most compatible with a Monkey or Dragon, with a little effort can get along with a Rabbit or Cock, but have definite antipathy for a Horse.

Famous Rat people include...

Lauren Bacall (1924)
Pablo Casals (1876)
Ronald Reagan (1912)
Adlai Stevenson (1900)
Humphrey Bogart (1900)

YEAR OF THE OX

**1901, 1913, 1925, 1937,
1949, 1961, 1973**

A brainy type, extremely alert mentally, you inspire confidence in others, and are a leader rather than a follower. Ox people make remarkably good parents.

You have endless patience and tend to be quiet even when violently opposed — but when you do converse you have something worthwhile to say.

Security is your thing. You worry about it a great deal. If you have this all-important security you are likely to lead a solid, quiet life, regarded by others as a pillar of society with staunch qualities.

You like people but can live happily alone because of your strength of character. Those born in the year of the Ox have a peculiar attitude toward marriage. Not particularly passionate, your aloofness can make for misunderstandings with your mate. Yet Ox women are unusually feminine — and Ox men have a rare understanding of women.

Your main fault is stubbornness and a narrowness of outlook that prevents you from adopting new ideas. Failure is maddening to you; it is the one wrinkle in life that will certainly cause you to lose your temper.

Your best bet as a marriage partner is the Snake or the Cock. Beware of the Sheep —the worst possible relationship for you.

Famous Ox people include...

Charlie Chaplin (1889)
Adolph Hitler (1889)
Richard Nixon (1913)
Gary Cooper (1901)
Lloyd Bridges (1913)

YEAR OF THE TIGER

**1902, 1914, 1926, 1938,
1950, 1962, 1974**

Tiger people make the world go round.
You aim straight for your goal with great
courage; in point of fact, it is difficult for
you to compromise because of your ag-
gressiveness.

You are intense and quite candid, and
others know precisely where they stand
with you. You have great warmth and a
sparkling personality, a combination re-
sulting in devoted friends.

The admiration of others is vitally necessary to you because of a somewhat overblown opinion of yourself. This vanity must be fed, otherwise you become unhappy.

Your sensitivity makes you very sympathetic to others, yet you are frequently short tempered and stubborn. You tend to be suspicious of people's motives, a trait which is perhaps responsible for the fact you find it difficult to make decisions.

While your middle life is the most difficult and old age should be serene, your inability to sort out important matters may well extend your troubles into your later life.

For mates and friends, look for the Dog and the Horse. You'll argue with the Snake and Boar —and do well to bypass the Monkey.

Famous Tiger people include...

Dwight Eisenhower (1890)
Marilyn Monroe (1926)
Nijinsky (1890)
Alec Guinness (1914)
Oscar Wilde (1854)

YEAR OF THE RABBIT

**1903, 1915, 1927, 1939,
1951, 1963, 1975**

You are easily the luckiest of all 'year people' — talented and articulate. Lucky also at finance, your hunches pay off on investments. You have a fine mind for business.

Extremely affectionate, you are often too shy to show this side of your nature, but it evidences itself in your 'green thumb' with others. An innate nourisher of life, you work particularly well with sick or unhappy people, always ready with a shoulder for them to cry on. Nursing or welfare would be ideal as careers.

A placid nature will take you through life on an easy course. You have many admirers because of your good taste and reserve. Diplomatic and tactful, you are looked upon as a peacemaker.

You are fond of those who are your cup of tea, but tend to ignore people not your own type. Tears come easily, and you often take things too personally.

As you are extremely possessive by nature you should try not to smother those you love.

You also tend to complain a lot, but withal, the aim and keystone of your life is peace, and all three phases of your existence should be happy ones.

Marry a Sheep or Boar, watch for conflict with the Dragon and the Rat. The Cock is your opposite and may bring trouble.

Famous Rabbit people include...

W. C. Fields (1879)
Albert Einstein (1879)
Bob Hope (1903)
Hedy Lamarr (1915)
Yul Brynner (1915)

YEAR OF THE DRAGON

**1904, 1916, 1928, 1940,
1952, 1964, 1976**

There's an aura of mystery about you. The Dragon is the most eccentric of the animal years. No one is sure exactly how you will react to a situation or what you will say — and you yourself enjoy this ambience.

Your purpose in life is complex; you want power, but instead of attacking your goal head on will go around the block and use a flank attack. Although you have a healthy respect for logic, you'll often defeat your own ends by acting on a last-minute hunch.

Dragon people, both men and women, have passionate natures and are very attractive to the opposite sex. Yet they tend to appear distant and elusive, which often destroys a romance.

You are blessed with unusual health, as the Dragon symbolizes the greatest celestial power.

No self-respecting Dragon will be caught making flowery speeches, but they are sincere, have strong opinions, are honest, brave, and inspire trust.

As a Dragon, you worry a lot for no particular reason, and are apt to be taken advantage of by others because despite your cool exterior you are in reality very soft-hearted.

You tend to be excitable and often say many things you don't mean. You take a strange delight in everything bizarre and for this reason sometimes incur the distrust of others.

You are not prone to marry early in life, perhaps not at all. Your early life is sometimes troubled because of your fastidious nature, your middle years are a series of ups and downs, and your old age should bring contentment.

You get along best with the Rat and Monkey, less with the Ox and Sheep, least of all with the Dog.

Famous Dragon people include...

Ingrid Bergman (1916)
Sigmund Freud (1856)
Nietzche (1844)
Cary Grant (1904)
Florence Nightingale (1820)

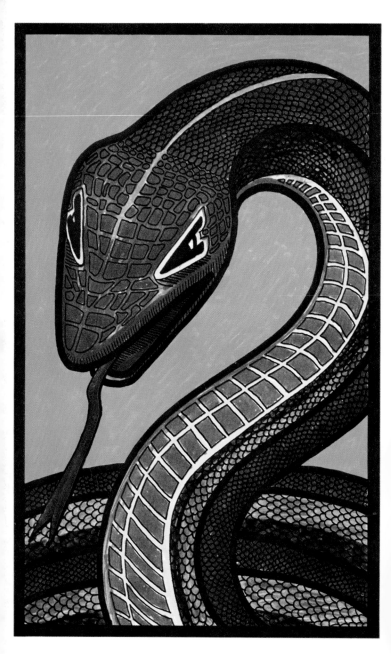

YEAR OF THE SNAKE

1905, 1917, 1929, 1941, 1953, 1965, 1977

You are among the wise people of the world. Deep and intense, you may not be blessed with a silver tongue, but when you speak you are worth listening to, for you possess tremendous wisdom.

Snake people tend to be beautiful physically, and if not, always use their potentials to the fullest. Passionate, they have a marvelous capacity to enjoy physical love, but often ruin a marriage because of philandering.

You are strong-willed, terribly determined, have fine organizational powers, and should work in medicine, politics, in any field where there is a sort of life-and-death urgency — the kind of life you thrive on.

On this score, you tend to go through life looking for the 'mission' you are positive you were put on earth to fulfill. You have enormous energy that needs an outlet, and until you discover what it is, you can be a nuisance to others (chip-on-the-shoulder type) and yourself.

You have great empathy for others and will go to any length to help. Here again you can be a nuisance, as you overdo everything—even in your good heartedness.

With your one-track mind, trying to hit your target, you seem to others stronger than you really are; actually you're vulnerable because of your sensitivity.

You tend to be vain, perhaps a bit foppish in your dress, are dreadfully obstinate, and have a simmering, seething temper that is quite frightening when aroused. You are your own worst enemy.

Most of your life, you'll be able to wiggle, like the snake, out of most troublesome situations. But take care, as your third phase will be your most difficult.

You have affinity with the Cock and Ox, so-so relationships with the Rat and Rabbit, and the worst possible with the Boar.

Famous Snake people include...

John F. Kennedy (1917)
Greta Garbo (1905)
Cole Porter (1893)
Mao Tse-tung (1893)
Karl Menninger (1893)

YEAR OF THE HORSE

1906, 1918, 1930, 1942, 1954, 1966, 1978

You come on strong, impress people with your cheer and sense of well being. Popular, naturally, because you spread joy.

Attracted strongly to the opposite sex, you can often lose all sense of balance when emotionally involved, allowing all other aspects of your life to fly to the winds. Yet in the workaday world you can be quite bored. Sitting around is not your idea of a good time, and you are so anxious to maintain your independence that you refuse advice of others, insisting on striking out on your own.

You are quick in everything you do, and good at working with your hands. Although not famous for patience, you are good at handling money.

Crowds attract you, and you love theater, sports arenas, any place where there's entertainment, excitement and people.

Subtlety is often lost on you. Your dress and manner is apt to be ostentatious, and you like a belly laugh better than a chuckle. You tend to talk too much, and sometimes too loudly, because you are so over zealous. A little discretion and humility would be an improvement.

Your life will be troublesome (slow down!) in the first two phases, but serene toward the end.

Marry a Dog or Tiger, who will understand that while you think you're happy alone, you really need people. And shun the Rat.

Famous Horse people include...

Carrie Nation (1846)
Igor Stravinsky (1882)
Audrey Hepburn (1930)
James Whistler (1834)
Rita Hayworth (1918)

YEAR OF THE SHEEP

**1907, 1919, 1931, 1943,
1955, 1967, 1979**

Elegance is your keynote — in dress, personality and life style. It therefore follows that you will be accomplished in the arts; at the very least you will be an avid buff.

Creative talent is the reason you will always earn enough money, all through your life, to satisfy your tastes.

On the surface it would seem your life is blessed with good fortune, but this is not entirely true. Because underneath your dazzling surface is an extremely shy nature — shy to the point that you are often unsure what direction to take.

Your timidity results in a need for guidance, but when led, you are deeply dedicated to your purpose and beliefs. You are probably a deeply religious person.

Wise and gentle, you have innate pity for those less fortunate than you — and when you give charity, which you are prone to do freely, you prefer to do it anonymously as gratitude would only embarrass you.

You allow very few people into your inner self, yet you are good at handling others and would do well in social activities or politics as you are very community minded.

As you advance through life you tend to become narrow-minded, and if not careful to keep receptive to change, you might well end up a definite square.

Great good fortune in your latter years follows a period filled with emotional problems.

The Rabbit and Boar are most compatible with you, but you could happily hate the Ox.

Famous Sheep people include...

Babe Ruth (1895)
Mitzi Gaynor (1931)
Kahlil Gibran (1883)
Jeanette MacDonald (1907)
Robert Young (1907)

YEAR OF THE MONKEY

1908, 1920, 1932, 1944, 1956, 1968, 1980

Monkey people are the geniuses—sometimes much too clever for their own good. You are such a charmer that everyone knows when you enter a room.

You have a nimble mind, immense good humor, are able to influence others easily—and if you have a personal disaster, are blessed with the knack of shrugging it off.

You have deep desire for knowledge, are an omnivorous reader, and so clever and skillful that you could be called the achiever of the cycle.

You tend to go after your goal of the moment with great enthusiasm, and if all goes well, you may well become famous. But you are easily bored, and if too many obstacles present themselves, you can leave a project in midstream and attack a new one.

Surpassingly original, you easily solve difficult problems, and are a near-genius in financial matters. You are flexible and talented, have a marvelous memory, yet are much too highly strung. You might well be the life of the party after every-one else has gone home.

You can make others feel they are im-portant, but in reality you are engrossed in your own affairs, and you frequently and secretly are contemptuous of others.

You are not a 'nester', preferring travel and adventure, and because you cool quickly, may well have difficulty in sticking to your marriage partner. It should be added that you are the cycle's most talented flirt.

Your best career would be in writing, teaching or advertising, but because you are so easily discouraged, your middle life is your worst—filled with confusion and interrupted plans.

Marry a Dragon or Rat, and avoid the Tiger.

Famous Monkey people include...

Elizabeth Taylor (1932)
Richard Burton (1920)
Eleanor Roosevelt (1884)
F. Scott Fitzgerald (1896)
Bette Davis (1908)

YEAR OF THE COCK

1909, 1921, 1933, 1945, 1957, 1969, 1981

You are filled with a pioneering spirit and will bravely sail over any new horizon. A thirst for knowledge leads you to broaden your mind through reading and travel.

Devoted to work, you labor almost for the sheer love of it, often planning in excess of your capabilities. You have great verve and self-confidence, and will do best in areas where enterprise, hard work and a good amount of nerve are necessary.

Despite your aspirations and your tendency for deep thinking, you can be improvident because you bite off more than you can chew, with the results that your fortunes all through life waver between good and bad.

Your emotions swing the same way, from one extreme to another. This eccentricity makes it difficult for you to maintain easy relationships with others. Your friendships often develop rough edges.

You seem able to achieve your aims by using the qualities of others, yet paradoxically, you prefer to be alone when engaged in your favorite pursuits.

As for your faults, you are overly sure you are right, and frequently unheeding of others' feelings. You find it difficult to laugh at yourself, a lack that leads to exaggerated self-importance.

Inasmuch as you will not brook interference in your ambitions, you would do well to marry an understanding Snake or Ox, and avoid the Rabbit.

Famous Cock people include...

Katharine Hepburn (1909)
Rod McKuen (1933)
Deborah Kerr (1921)
Thornton Wilder (1897)
Flip Wilson (1933)

YEAR OF THE DOG

**1910, 1922, 1934, 1946,
1958, 1970, 1982**

As might be expected, Dog people are loyal, dependable, have a deep sense of duty. Their attitude toward others can be summed up as patient, tender and protective.

You are one of those rare human beings who can keep a secret and so inspire the confidence of others. This, combined with your honesty, gains for you the admiration of those around you—and you should therefore work extremely well with others.

While you are seldom a leader, you do very well as a second in command, and large business firms would do well to hire people born in the year of the Dog.

Although generous in praise of others, you tend to find fault with situations—or people who irk you. Aroused, you will have a remarkably sharp tongue and are a whiz at sarcasm.

It is perhaps this talent for the verbal caustic that is your only emotional outlet. You keep your temper quite well, to your own disadvantage, as the emotion boils inside you almost constantly.

You are sometimes underrated by those around you as you are not good at small talk and therefore a wallflower at social gatherings. Your sense of humor, gentle and quiet, leads others to think of you as a plodder.

You are stubborn and a bit selfish, distant socially and emotionally cool in private, although you can be most amorous. Your best attribute is as a friend, dependable and comfortable as an old shoe.

Your greatest affinity is with the Tiger or Horse, and you will have antipathy for the Dragon.

Famous Dog people include...

Winston Churchill (1874)
Ava Gardner (1922)
Robert Frost (1874)
Edith Wharton (1862)
George McGovern (1922)

YEAR OF THE BOAR

**1911, 1923, 1935, 1947,
1959, 1971, 1983**

You are the campaigner of the cycle. You almost *have* to have a cause to fight for. Like the knights of old, you have an inner strength to be devoted to good, and you are never so happy as when you are fighting for an underdog.

Chivalrous and gallant, you feel you must dig up the truth, and go at it whole hog, if you'll pardon the pun.

Trouble sometimes springs from all this nobility of purpose, because you concentrate so single-mindedly on your goal that you let everything else slide. When this happens, your life is likely to collapse into a shambles. You may even—and this is the truth—grow fat.

In trouble, you will not seek help from others, but try to solve it all yourself. In point of fact, you tend to look down on those less clever than yourself.

You make few friends, but those you have are lifelong, and fortunate to count you as one unrelentingly on their side.

You talk little, but when a subject interests you, you pour it all out endlessly, sometimes to the boredom of others. In brief, you are prone to be all or nothing at all, and so could be more boring to a partner than you really are. To avoid this, keep yourself interested in a wider scope of affairs.

You dislike arguments, are kind and affectionate, yet will have marital problems, with difficulties in your first and second phases of life.

Above all, stay out of court. You are much too honest and impulsive and will lose to a clever opponent.

You are most compatible with the Rabbit and Sheep. And you will do well to avoid marriage with another Boar.

Famous Boar people include...

Judy Garland (1923)
Ernest Hemingway (1899)
Lucille Ball (1911)
Fred Astaire (1899)
June Allyson (1923)